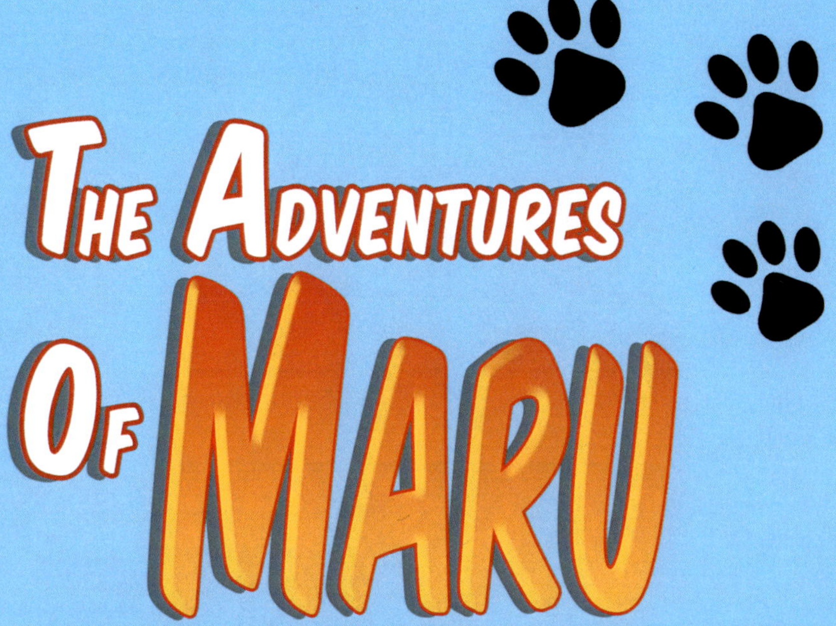

The Adventures Of Maru

Written by

Ashti A. Motilall

Published in the United States of America

ISBN 978-1-962110-73-0 (SC)
ISBN 978-1-962730-70-9 (HC)
ISBN 978-1-962730-91-4 (Ebook)

Motilall Publishing
222 West 6th Street
Suite 400, San Pedro, CA, 90731
www.stellarliterary.com

Order Information and Rights Permission:

Quantity sales. Special discounts might be available on quantity purchases by corporations, associations, and others. For details, contact the publisher at the address above.

For Book Rights Adaptation and other Rights Permission.
Call us at toll-free 1-888-945-8513 or send us an email at
admin@stellarliterary.com.

DEDICATION

This book is dedicated to my family. Without you, Maru's life wouldn't be the same.

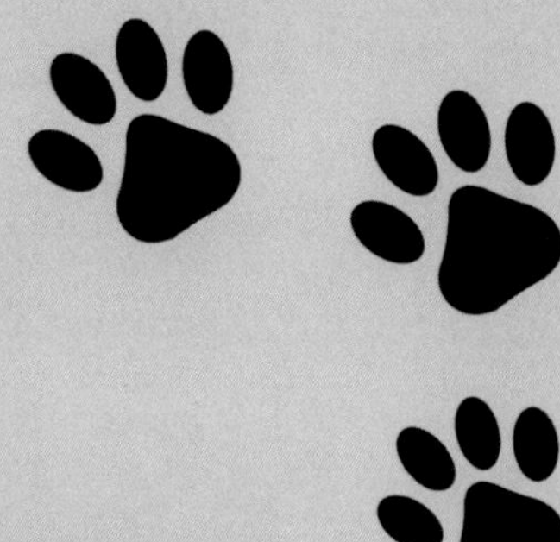

PREFACE

Maru was born in Minnesota on September 20th, 2019. Maru was separated from his husky family at a young age. He bounced around to a few different homes after his first owners' living situation didn't allow for them to take proper care of him any longer.

When Maru turned 6-months old, I saw a post about Maru needing a forever home. 24-hours later, Maru belonged to the Motilall family and all our lives were all greatly enhanced.

Maru brought joy into each family members' life at various stages over the past 3.5 years. He can be stubborn at times but he's silly, affectionate and a true companion.

I hope Maru continues to have many more adventures in the years to come. This book sets the stage for who Maru is, his life now, and all the things he loves.

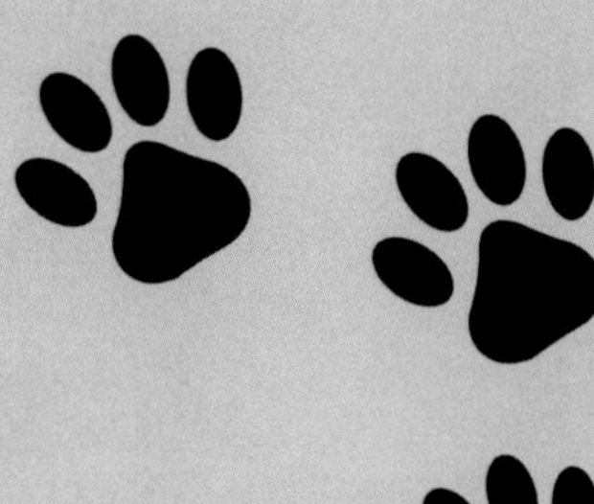

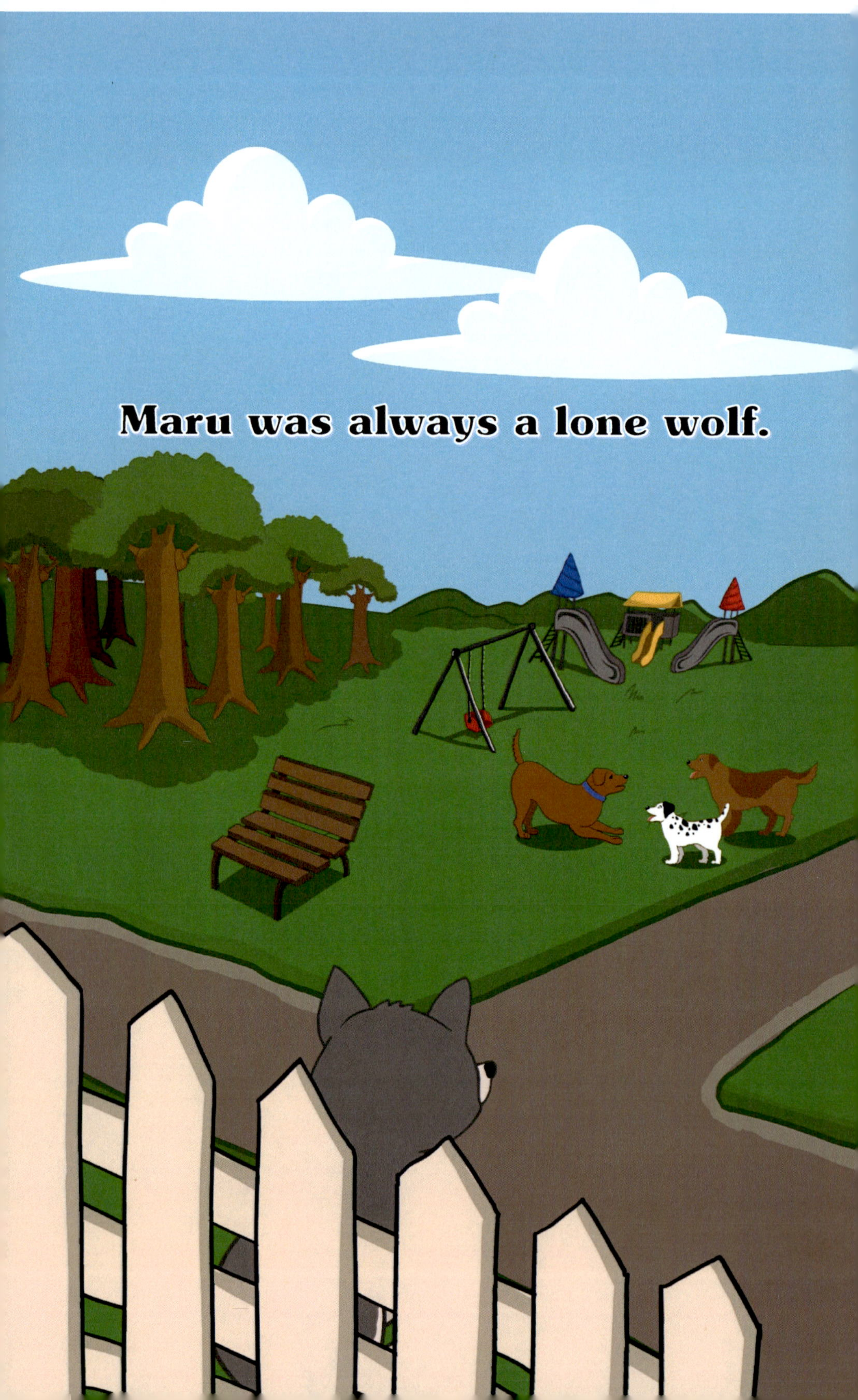
Maru was always a lone wolf.

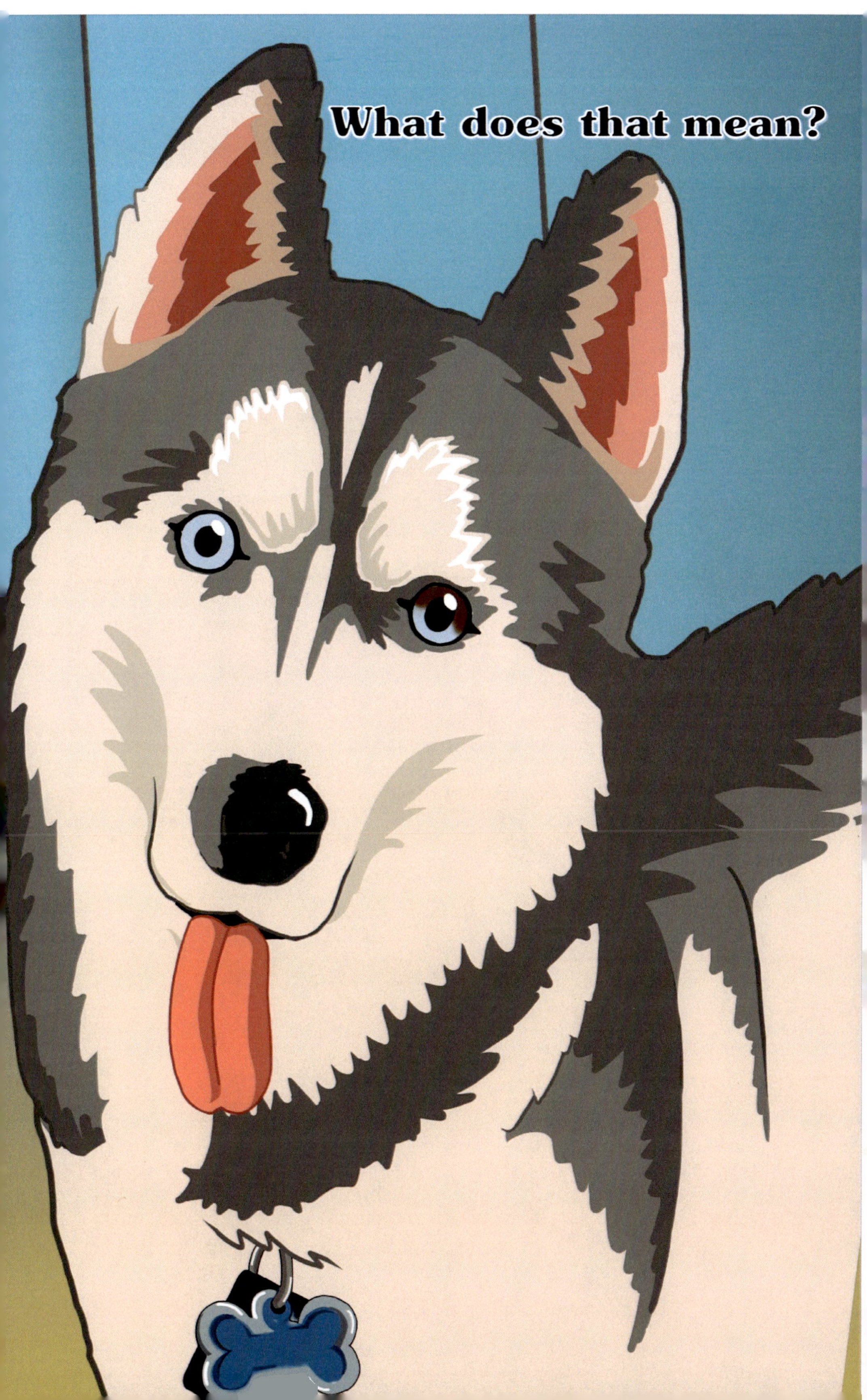
What does that mean?

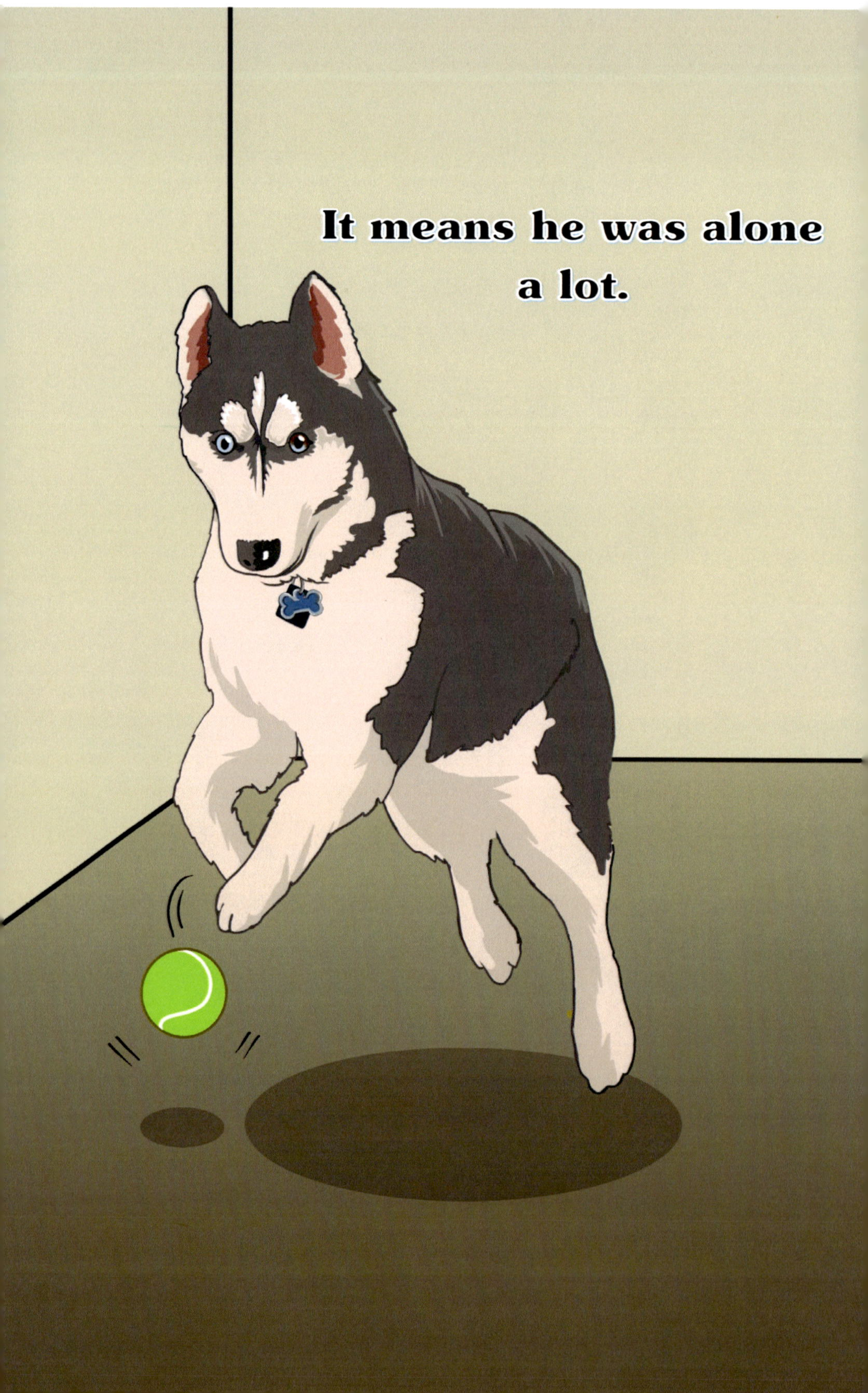
It means he was alone
a lot.

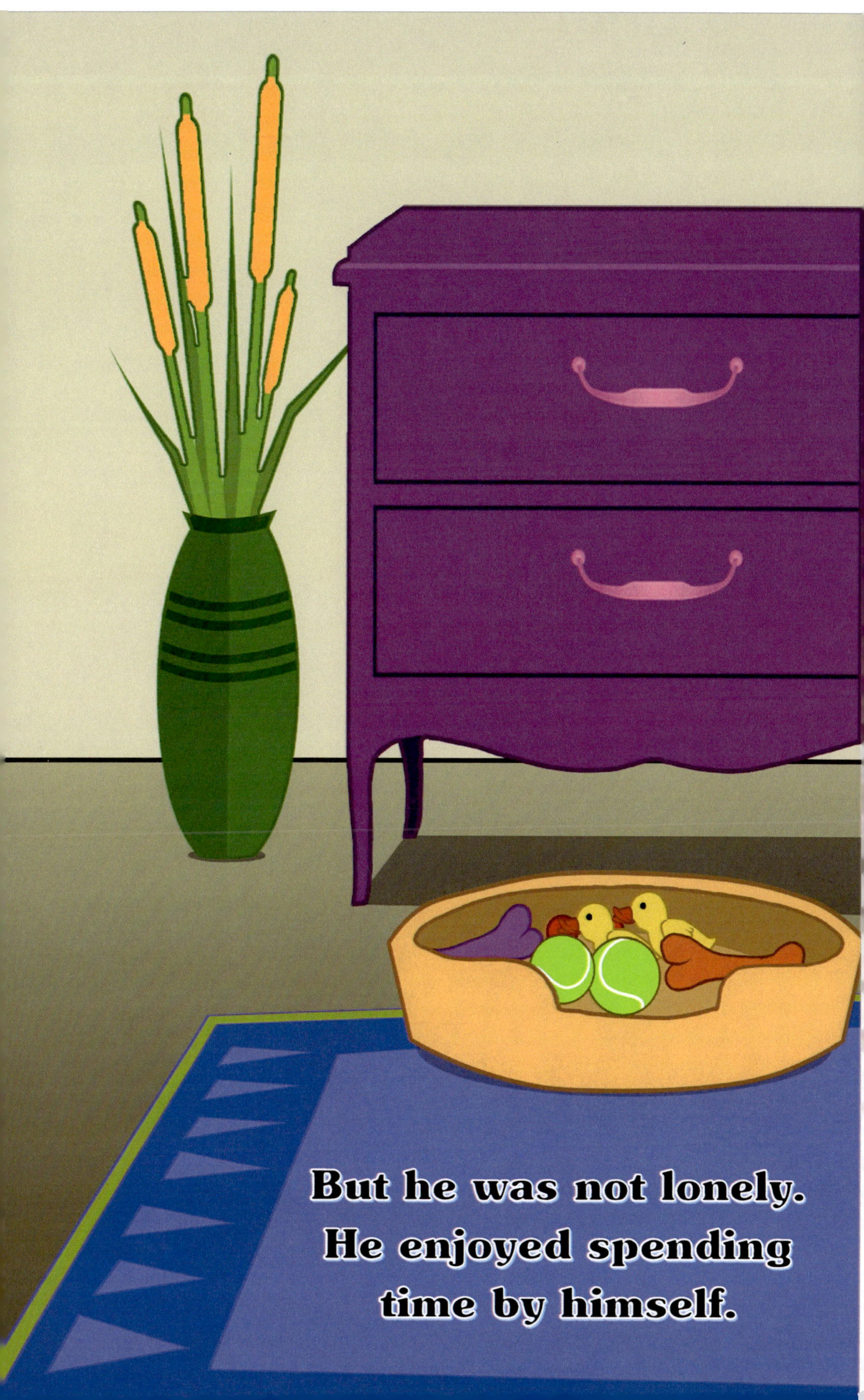

But he was not lonely.
He enjoyed spending
time by himself.

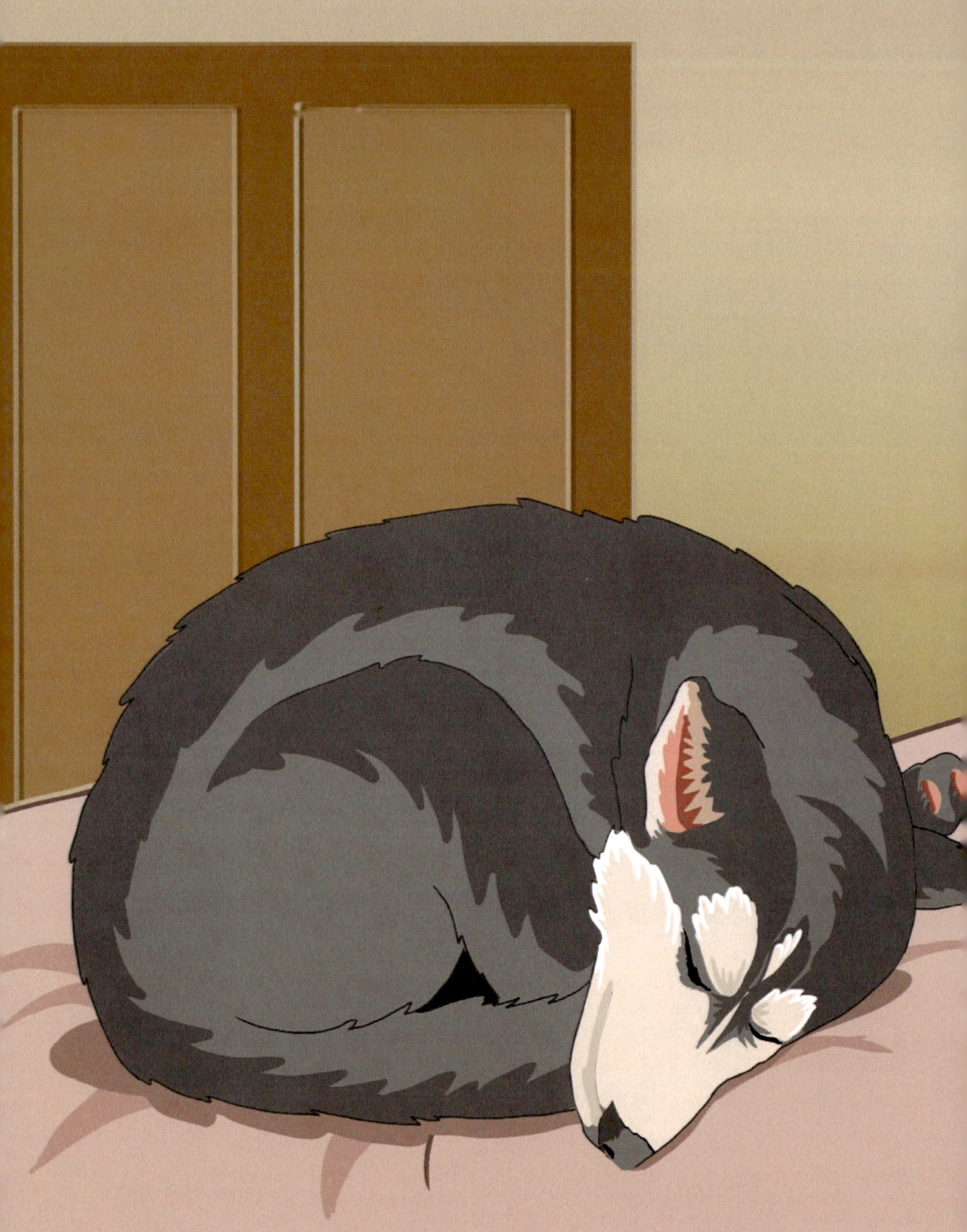

He could nap whenever
he wanted.

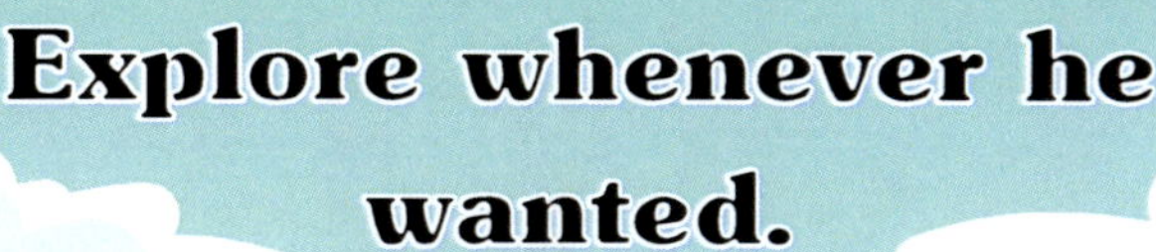

Explore whenever he
wanted.

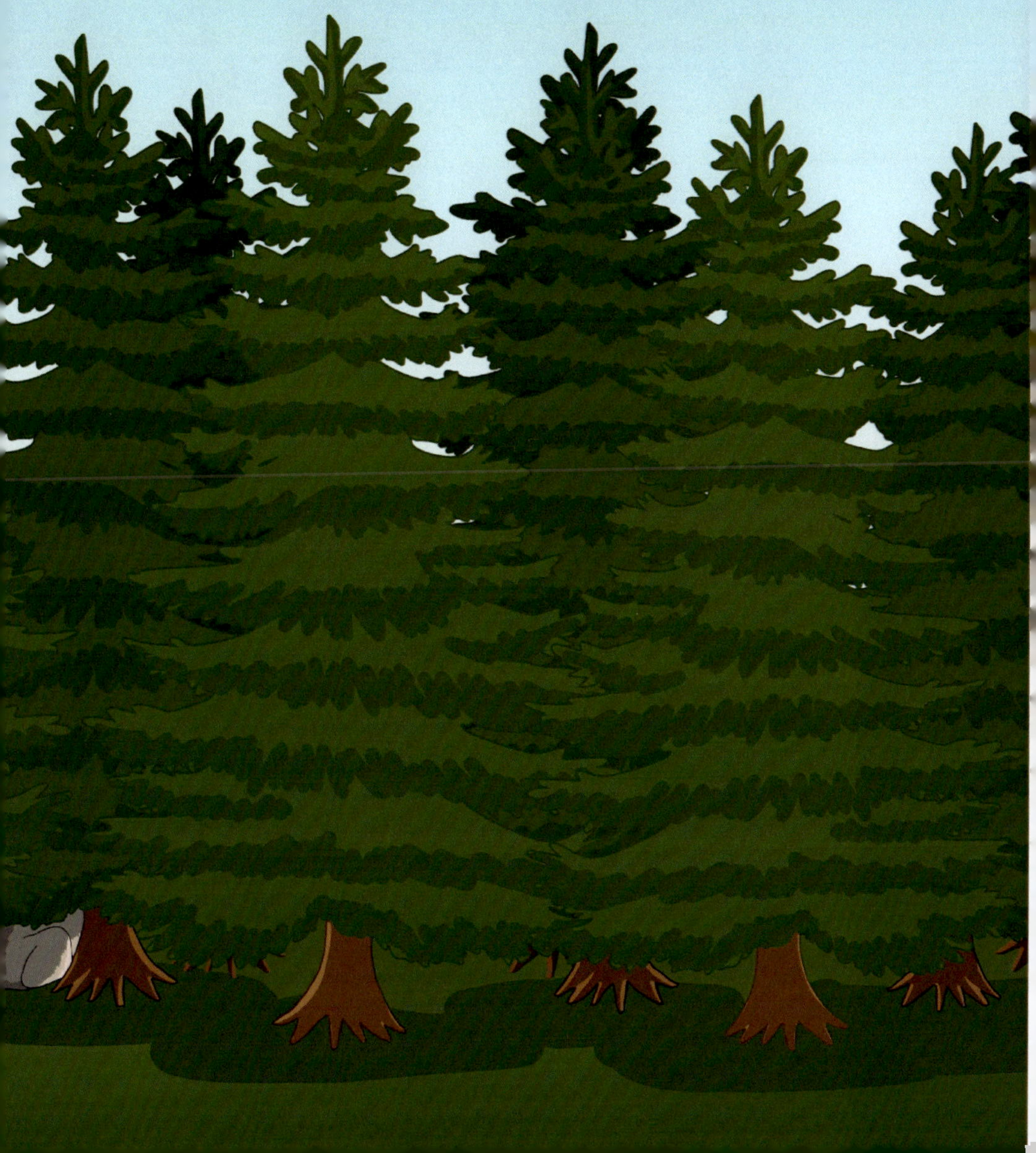

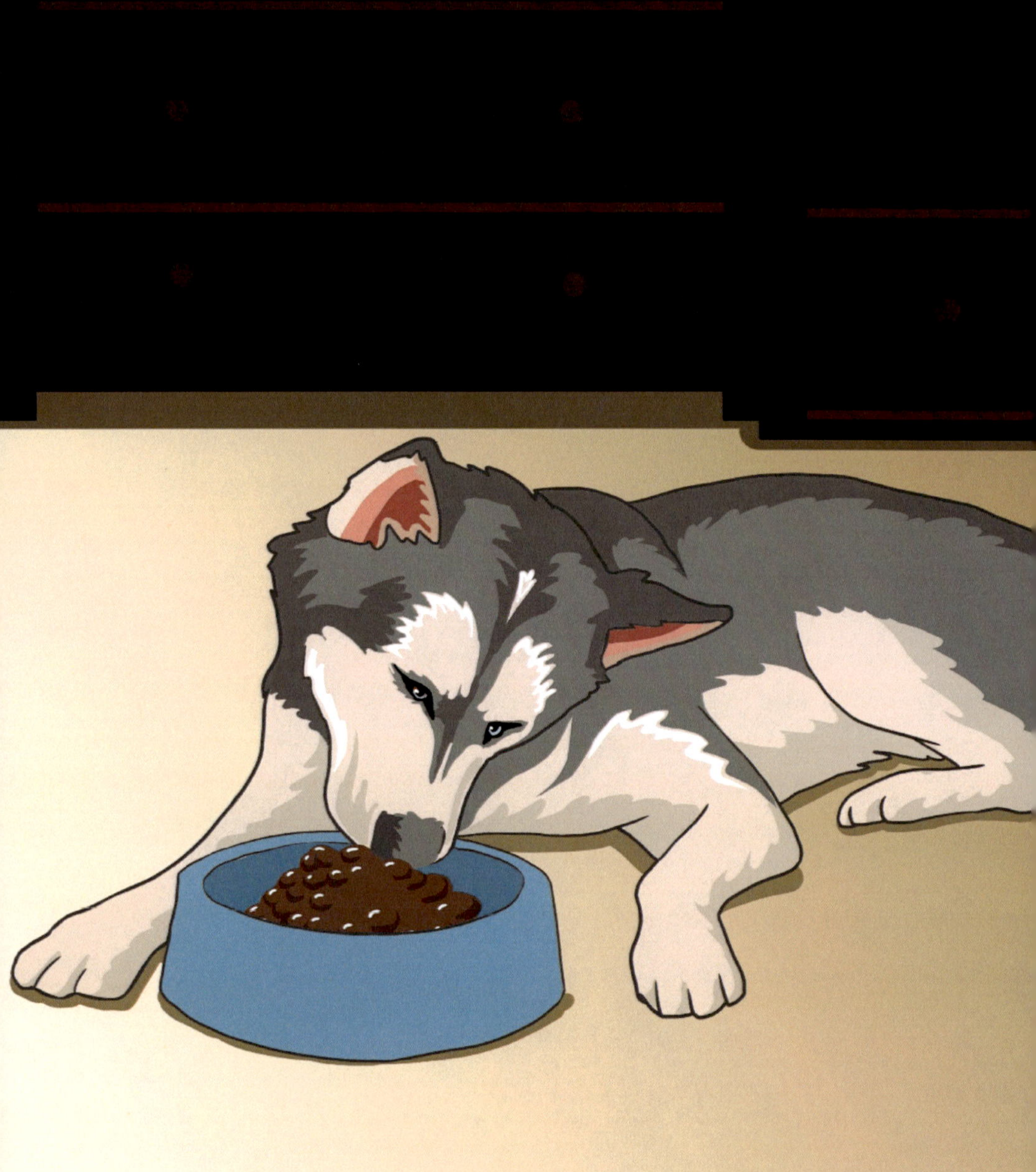

Eat whenever he wanted.

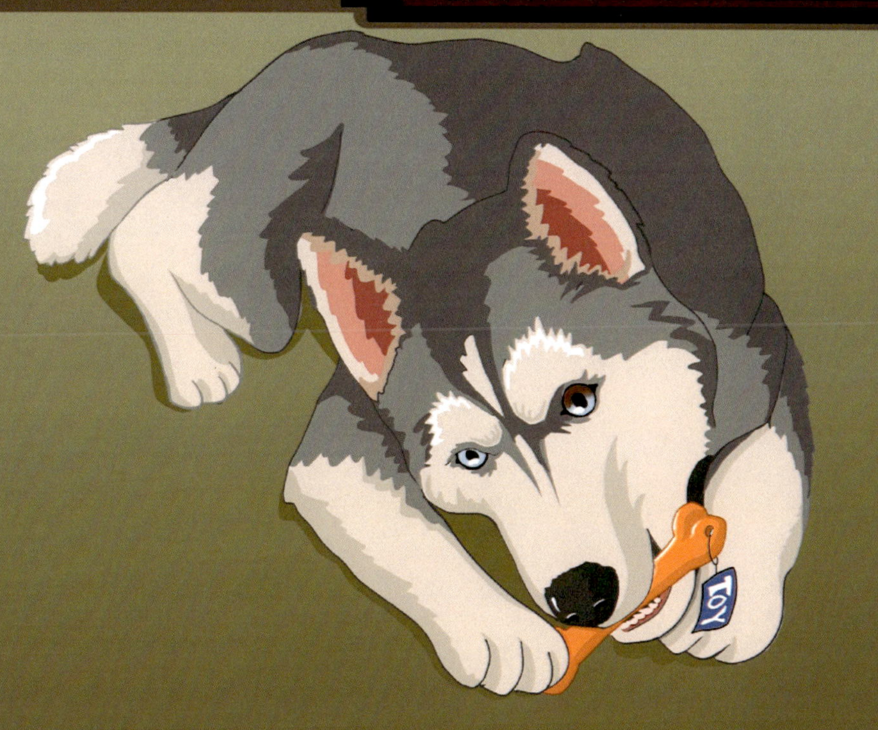

Play whenever he wanted.

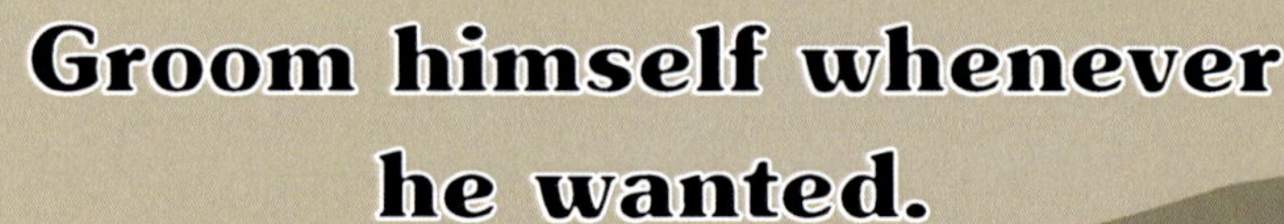

Groom himself whenever
he wanted.

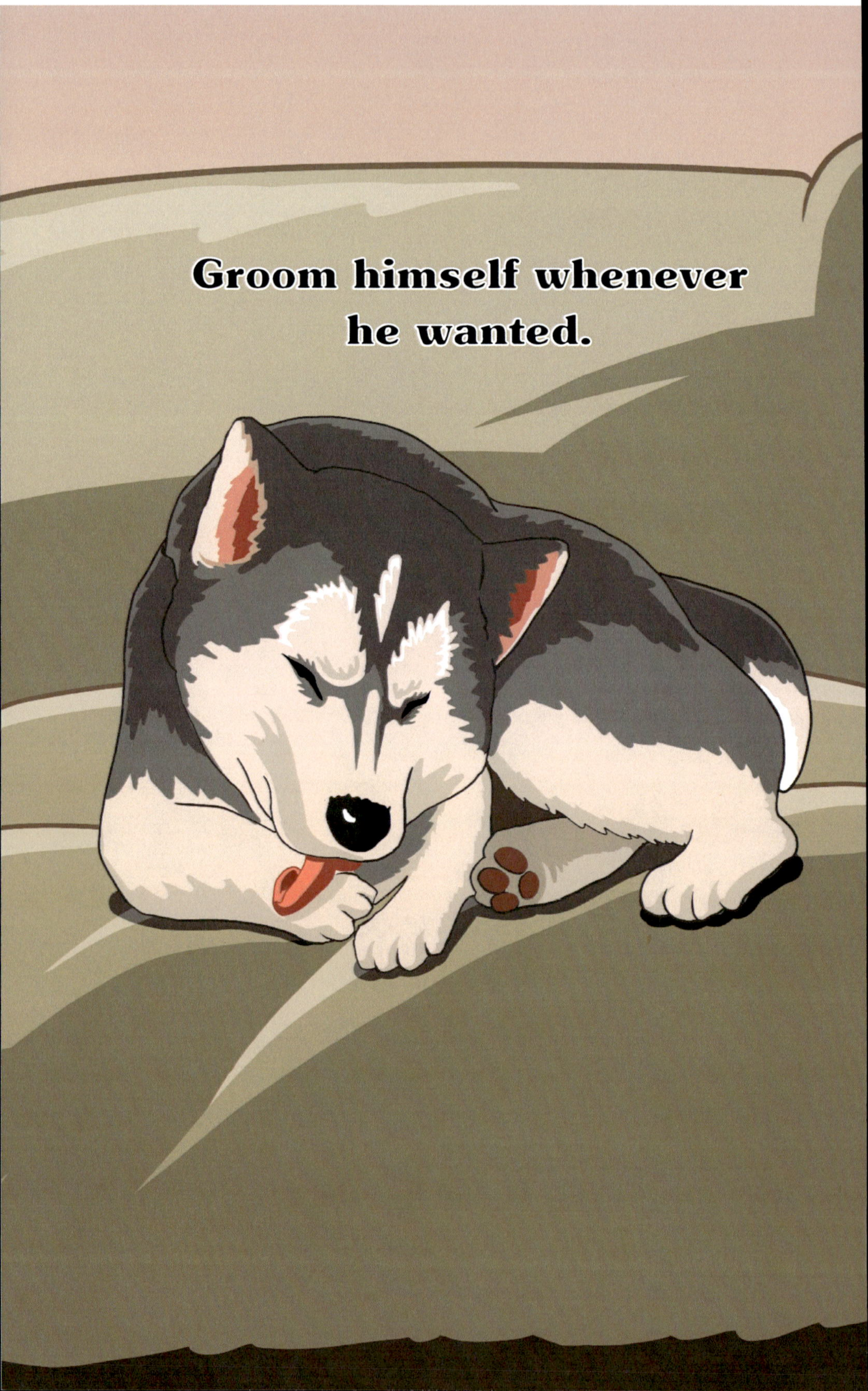

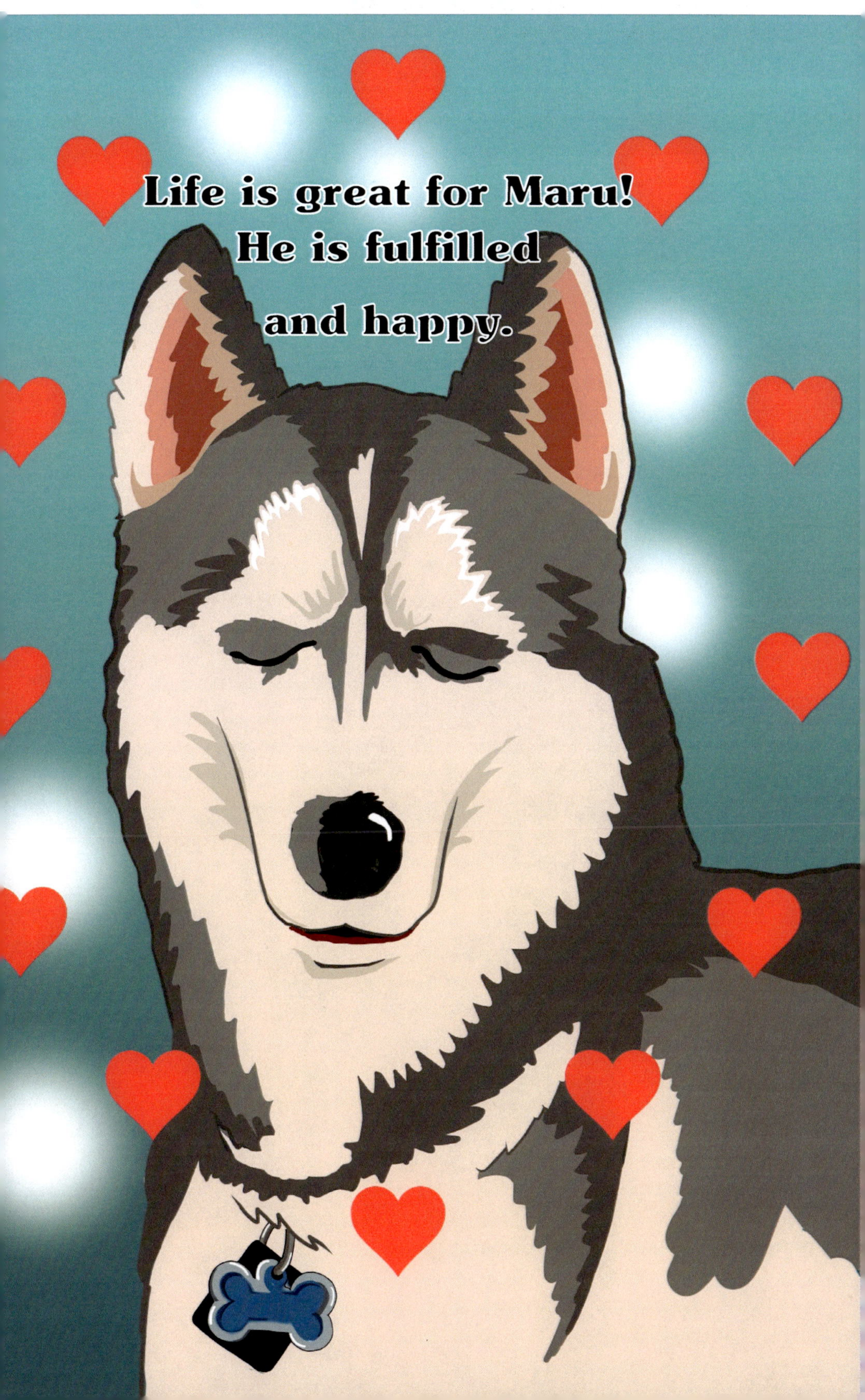

Life is great for Maru!
He is fulfilled
and happy.

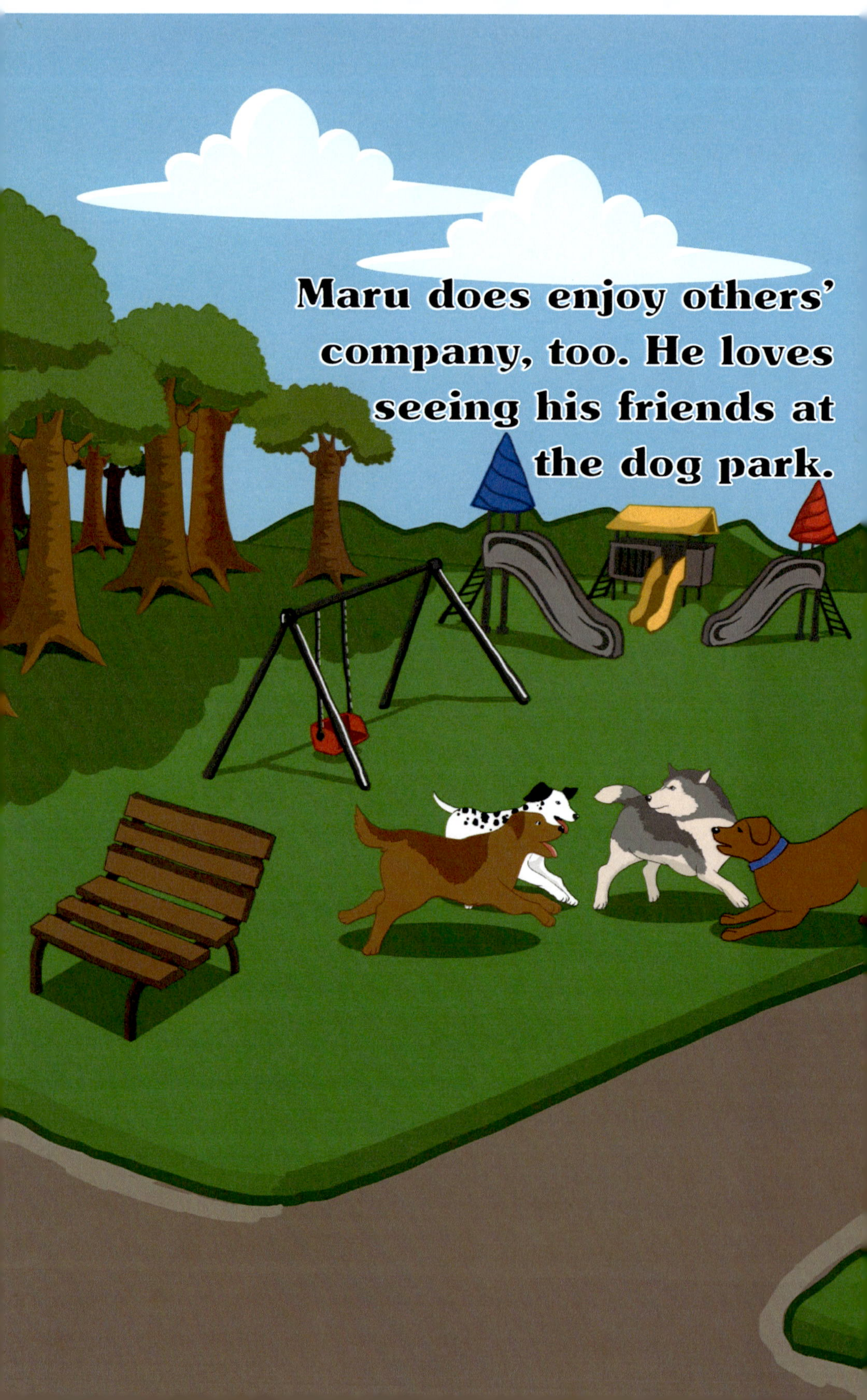

Maru does enjoy others' company, too. He loves seeing his friends at the dog park.

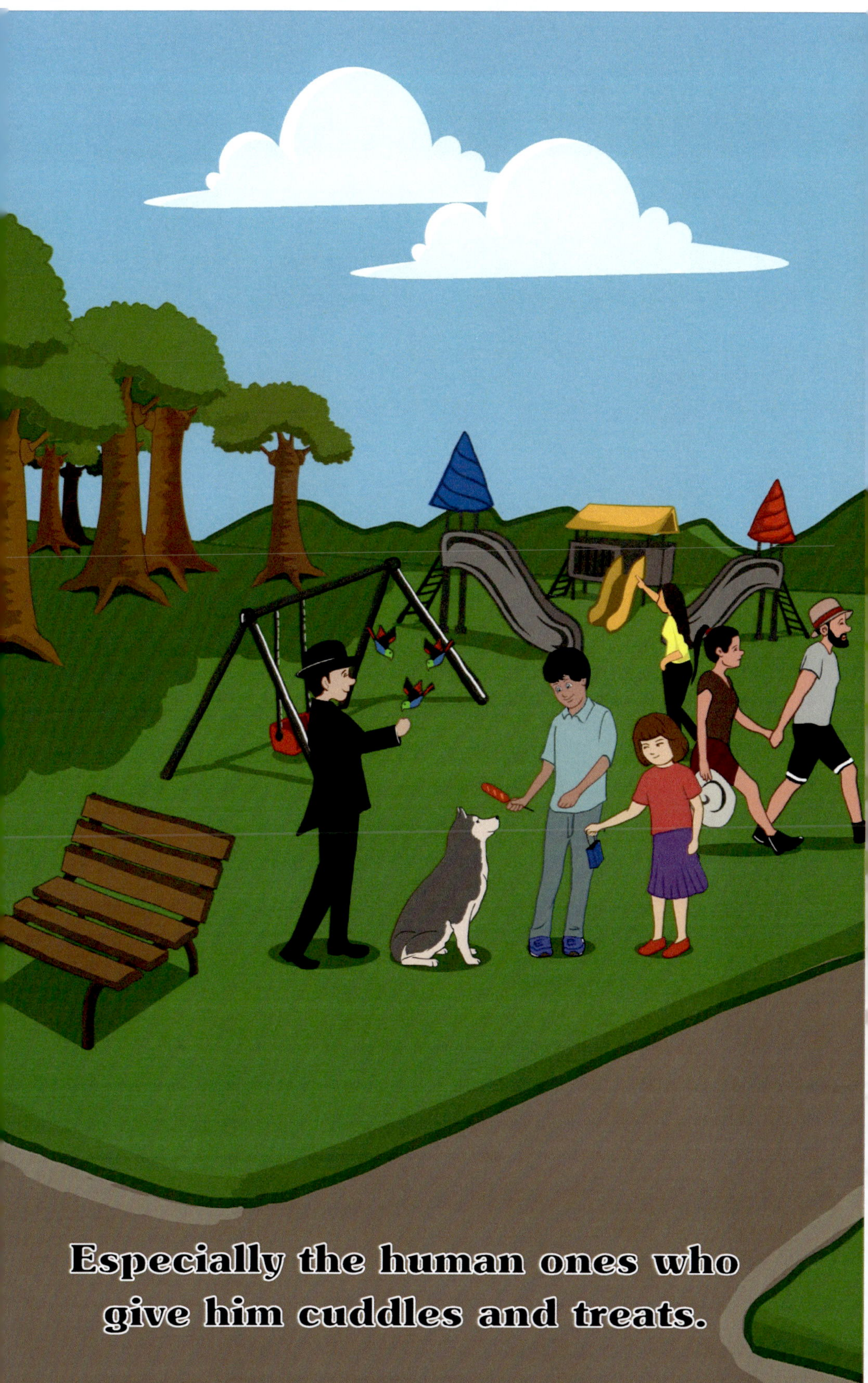

Especially the human ones who
give him cuddles and treats.

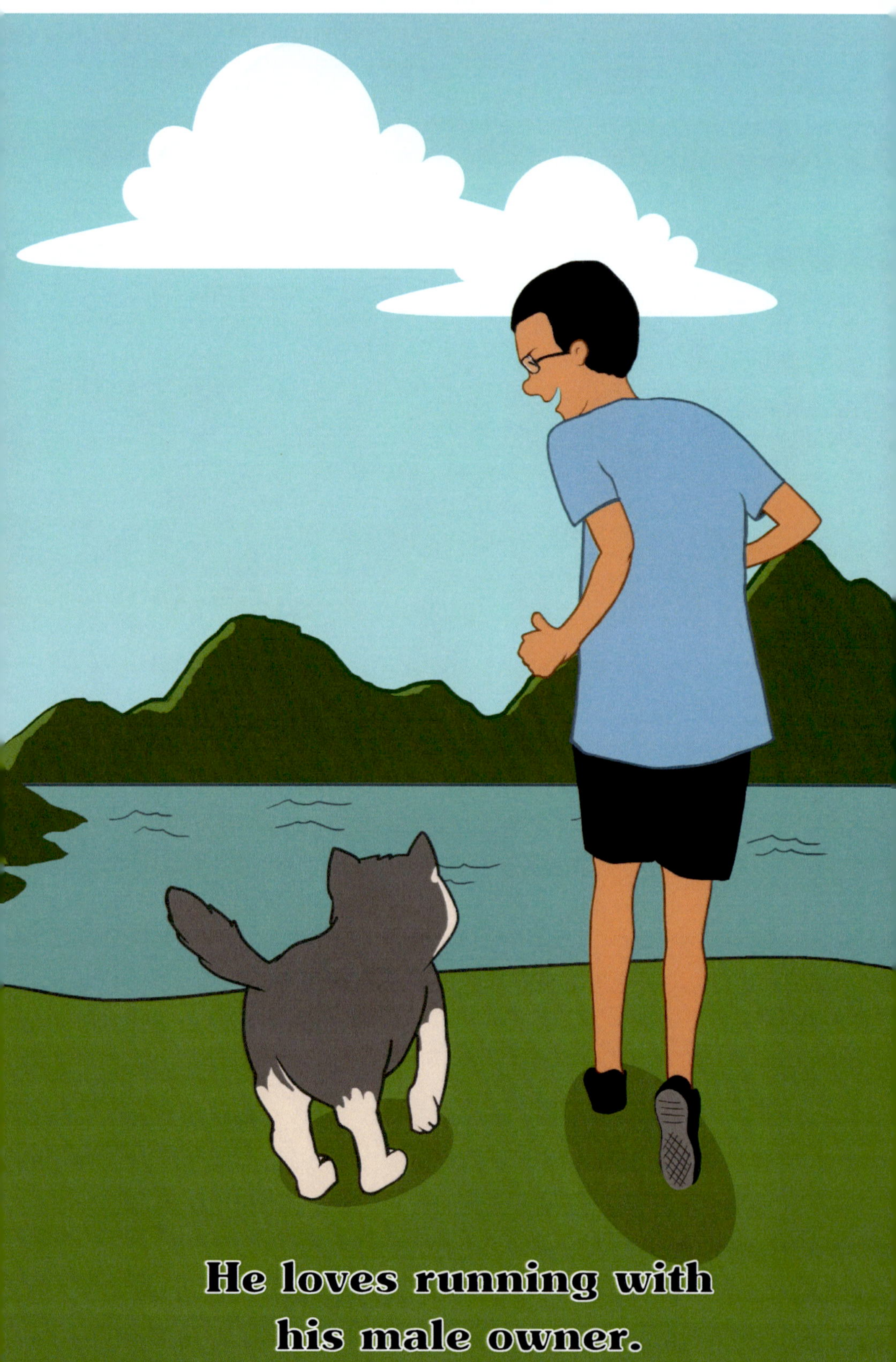

He loves running with
his male owner.

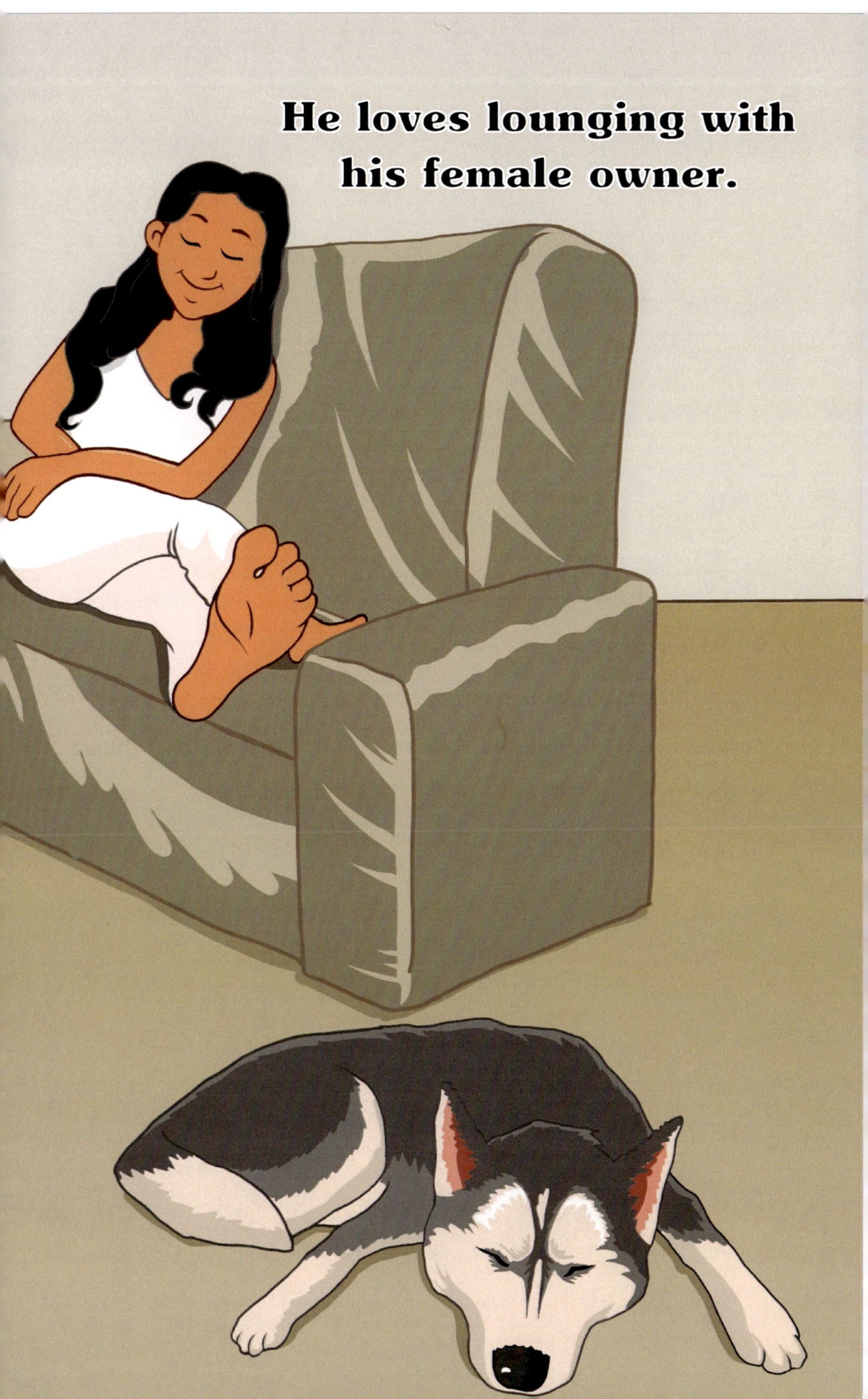
He loves lounging with
his female owner.

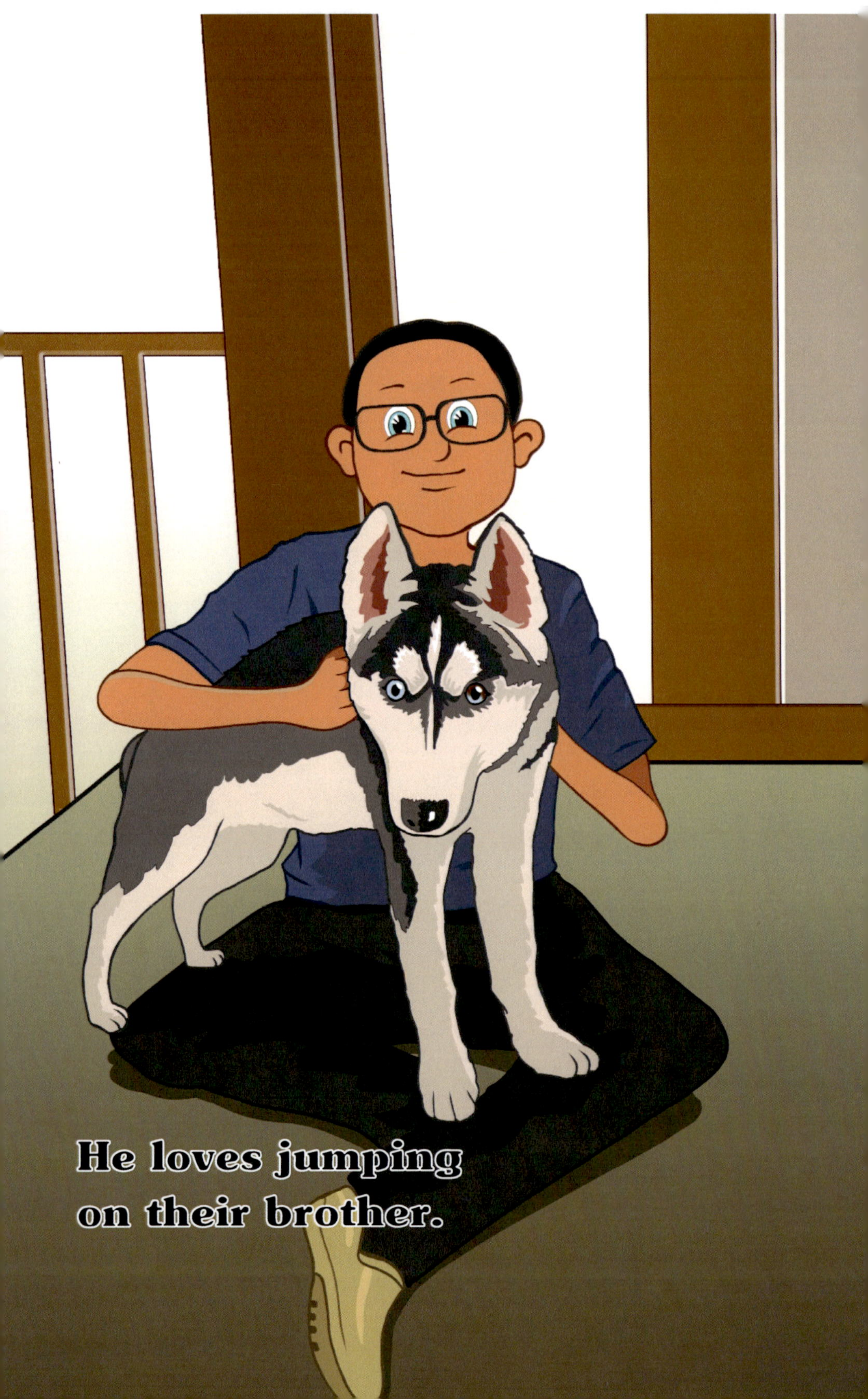
He loves jumping
on their brother.

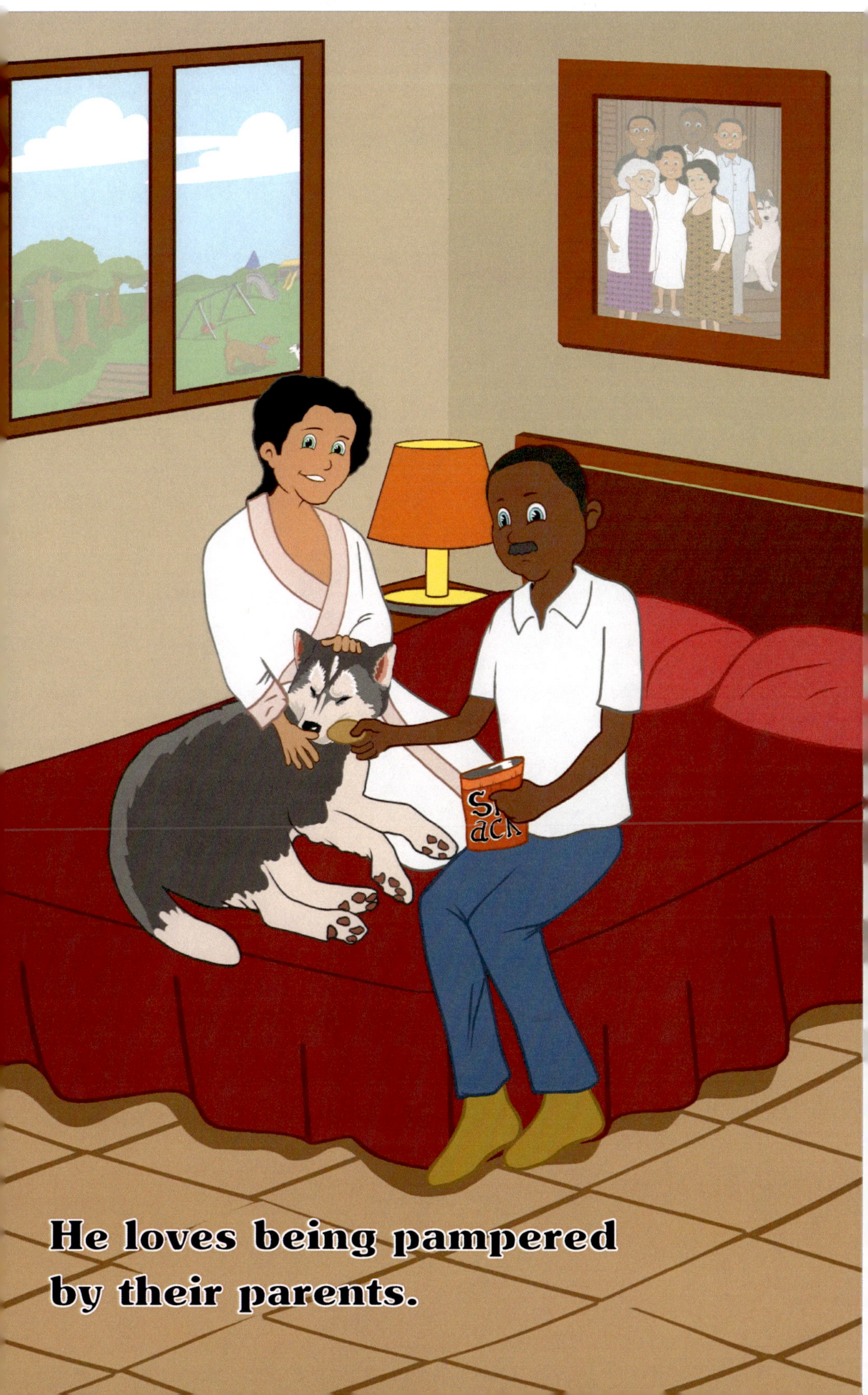

He loves being pampered
by their parents.

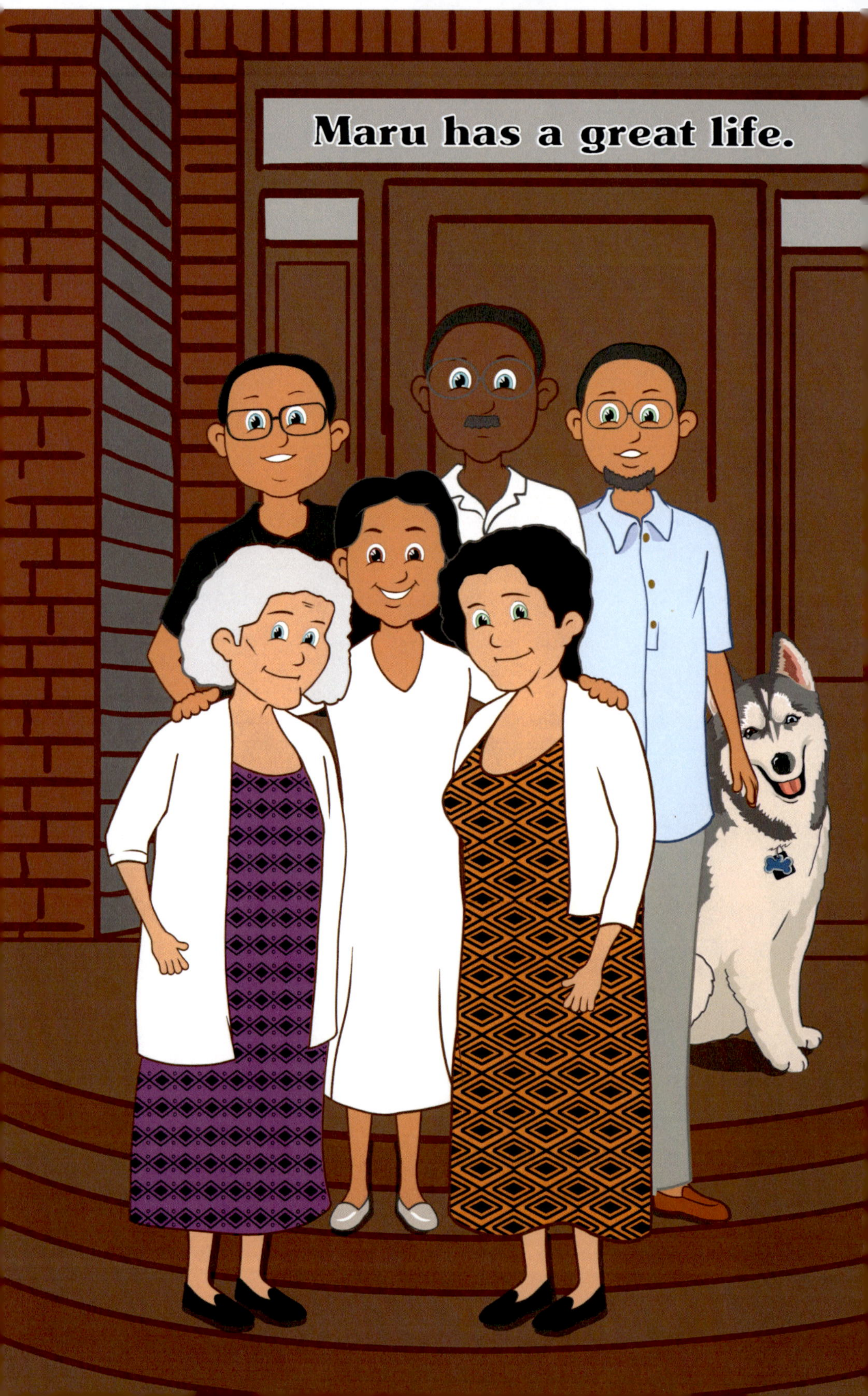
Maru has a great life.

Whether he is alone, with his family, or with his friends;

Maru is loved.

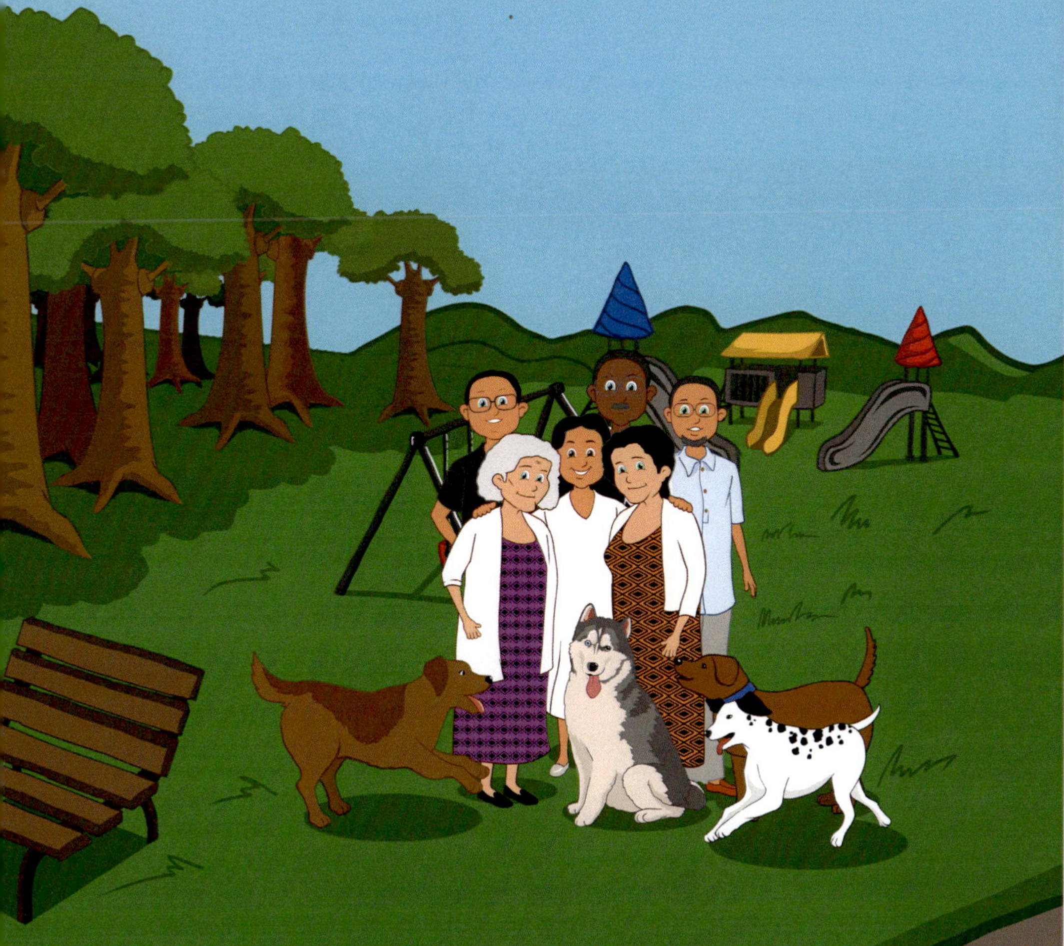

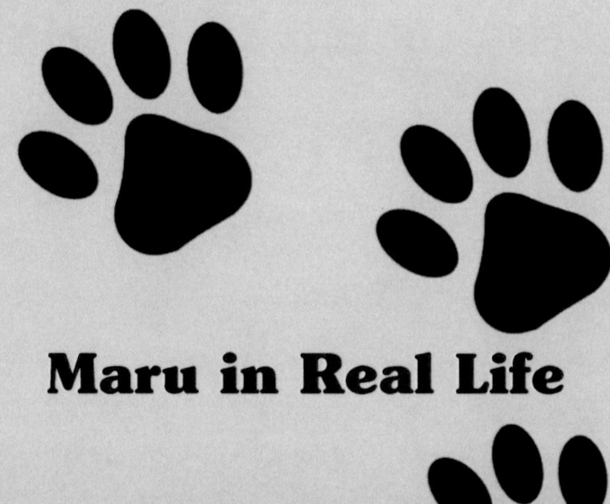

Maru in Real Life

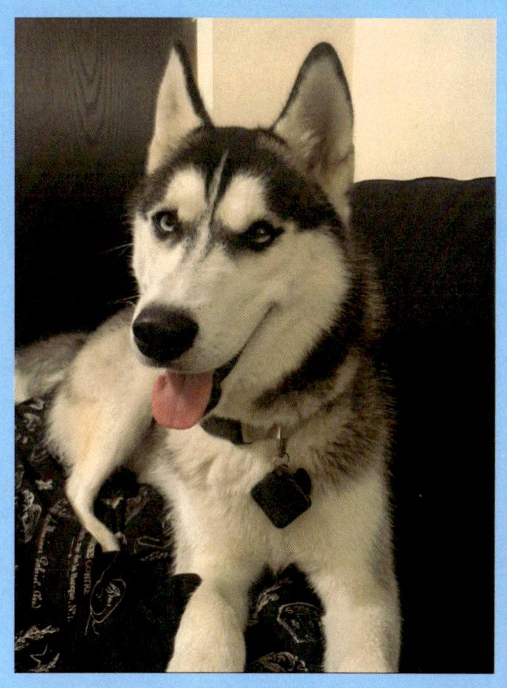
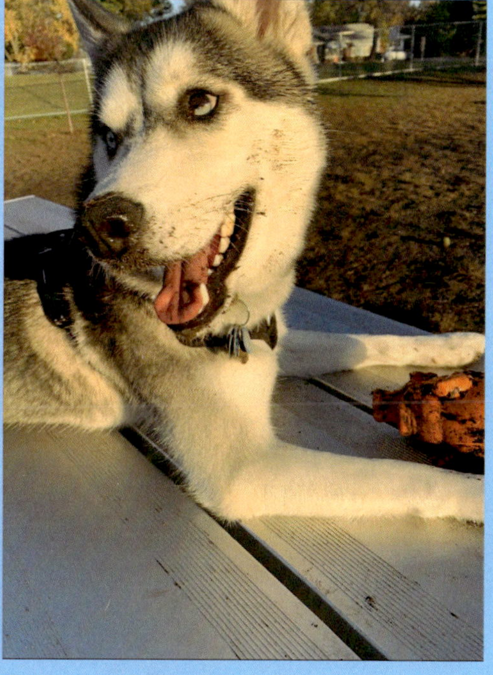
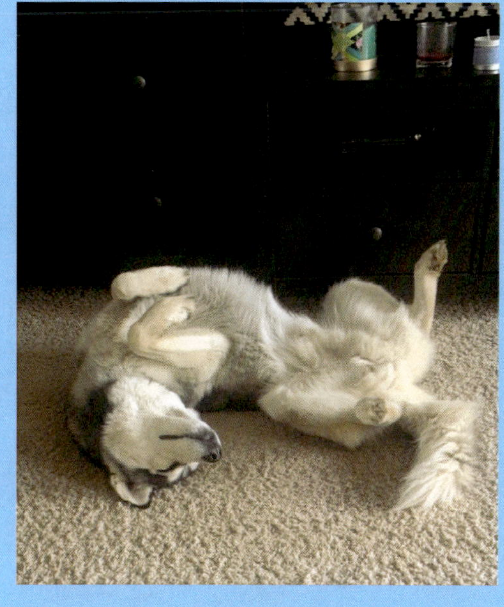
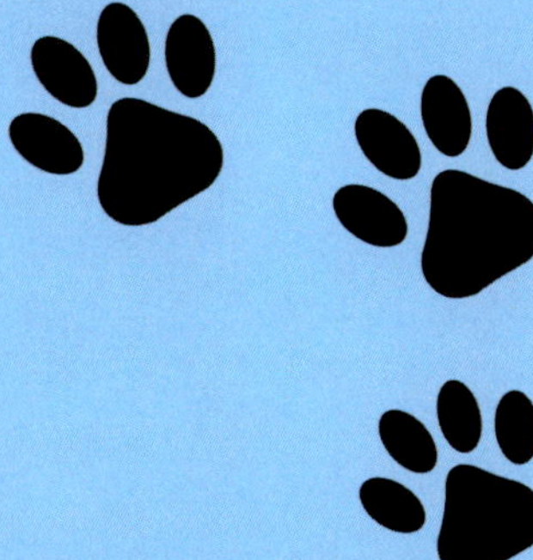

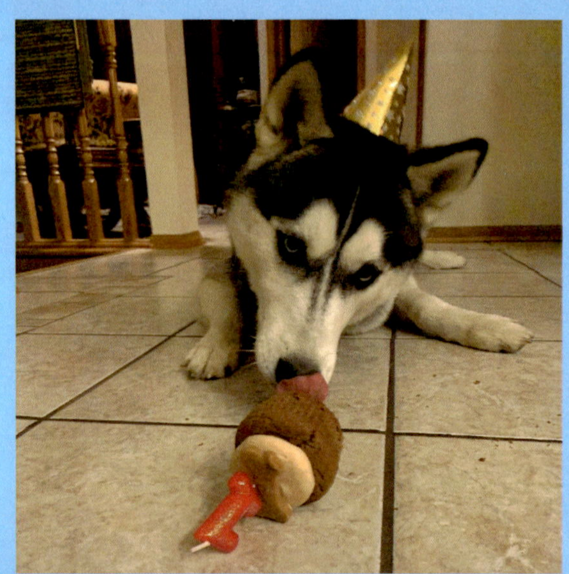

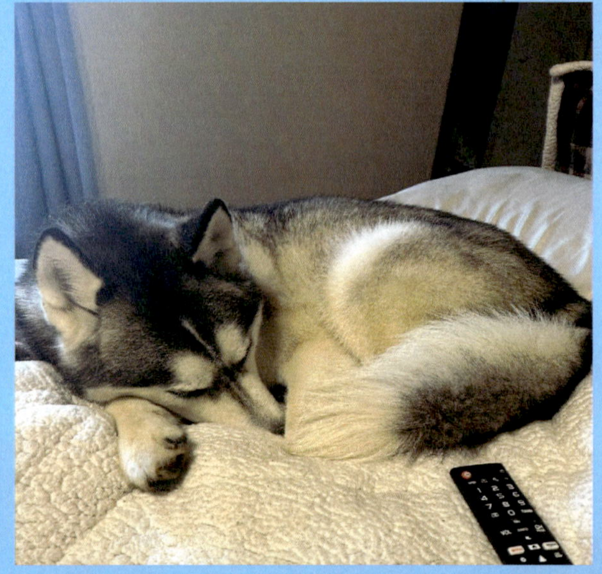

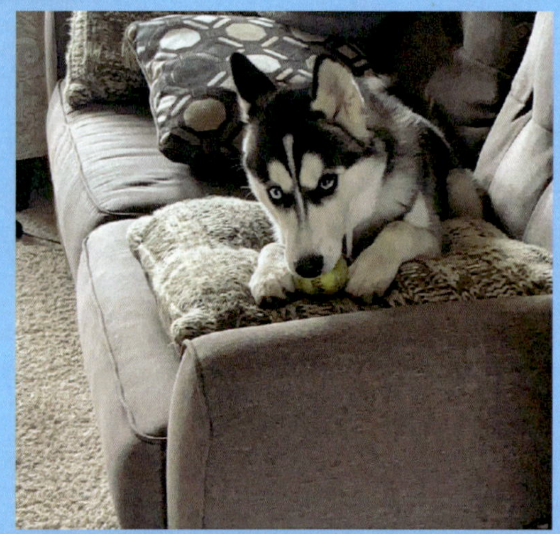